The Bamboo Effect:
Unleashing Your Potential
For "seemingly" overnight success

LEVEL SEVEN
ENTERPRISES

Melondy Waldrup Neal

The Bamboo Effect

ISBN: 978-0-9709423-6-4

Typesetting and Book Design
Tanya L. Streeter
Cover Design by Kimb Tiboni Manson
Level 7 Publishing

Printed in the United States

To Aaron and Jared, thanks for teaching me everything about pure love.

To my Mother, Gracie Brown:

Thank you for encouraging me to not be a one hit wonder.

A special dedication to Edwin D. Dunbar aka "Big Ed." Thank you for being one of the people who motivated me to graduate from Southern Arkansas University. In the words of Wynton Marsalis "We are going to miss you but we sure are glad we got to know you." Paradise Hill will always echo the stories of your life.

Table of Contents

Foreword

There are so many events in life, such as loss of employment, divorce or a natural disaster to name a few, which can **push** us to make immediate changes. Being forced out of our comfort zones can be somewhat liberating; however, the image of being pushed, while shocking at best, also brings with it opportunity. Many of us can probably remember facing a situation that made us ask questions such as, "What do I do now?"

That's the beauty of this book you're reading. By using the metaphor of a bamboo farmer, Melondy Waldrup Neal has managed to outline "how" to turn what looks like a crisis into an opportunity. I've had the pleasure of working with Melondy throughout the years on several projects. I've always been fascinated by how she rebounds from what appeared to be the direst of circumstances with such grace and seemingly effortless ability. Now I know how she did it and how she continues to successfully do it year after year with much skill and finesse. It's not magic, or rocket science, but rather simple principles that can be drawn upon at any time and made to work for anybody in any situation. She assures us that we all have the ability, or the "Good Farmer Skills" to start to control the direction of our lives in ways that we haven't considered before.

My hope for you is that you take away something from this book that will make changing a little less frightening. For me, it was that the only way to stop the feeling of failure was to embrace the fact this was my fifth year and grow!

Best regards,

Camellia R. Jackson, LCSW, LCDC

Camellia R. Jackson is a veteran of the United States Navy and a member of Alpha Kappa Alpha Sorority, Inc.

The Purpose and Mission

This book is simple, but the mission is huge. The sole purpose is to encourage and motivate everyone who reads it.

In February of 2012, I was fired from my job. I had never been fired in my entire working career. I started working when I was fifteen. Like most people who have lost a job, I was frightened, confused and worried about my future. I was a single mother responsible for everything. Having a job was mandatory. That was my thinking at the time. An amazing thing happened; after being unemployed for over six months and filling out application after application, I had an epiphany that would change my life forever. Being fired from my job was the push I needed. The loss of employment forced me to spread my wings and fly to a greater height. Yes, I needed to make money to support myself and my family; however, the ability to generate an income did not have to be in the traditional fashion I had been conditioned to adhere to since the age of fifteen. Before I knew it one year had passed without me finding employment. It was during this period of time, I discovered the story of the Chinese Bamboo plant. It instantly resonated with everything I knew to be true. It became my passion to share what I had discovered with

> "Everything happens for a reason."

people around the world. Yes, you can be successful. Yes, you can have wealth and prosperity. Yes, you can live a healthy life. Yes, you can find real love. We are all born with the potential to reach our destiny. It is just somewhere along the way we forget. *The Bamboo Effect* is a gentle reminder of the importance of tapping into the core of your truth and becoming the person you were born to be in the world.

If you are reading this book it is not by chance. I don't believe in random occurrences. As the old saying goes "Everything happens for a reason." There is no way for me to know your story. It is impossible for me to look into the eyes of each and every person who will read this and ask them "How did you get a copy of *The Bamboo Effect*?" Yet, as the spirit guides me to write these words, I have a calm assurance each and every copy will land in the hands of the very person(s) who needed it the most.

So before you read another word take a moment to feel special. Our answers to life's questions come in the strangest of sources. As you read this book, embrace its simplicity. It can be read in a single session. Yet, the power comes in implementing the messages into action.

The Story of Chinese Bamboo

You take a little seed, plant it, water it, and fertilize it for a whole year, and nothing happens.

The second year you water it and fertilize it and nothing happens.

The third year you water it and fertilize it and nothing happens. How disappointing and discouraging this becomes!

The fourth year you water it and fertilize it and nothing happens. This is more than you can bear.

The fifth year you continue your labor. You water it and fertilize the seed you planted many years before and then...the unexpected. Sometimes during the fifth year, the Chinese Bamboo tree sprouts and grows ninety feet into the air in six weeks.

The parable of the Chinese Bamboo has resulted in multiple lessons. As I studied this basic story, I asked "What lesson am I supposed to teach?" It became clear. It is not about the uniqueness of the bamboo shoot. It is not about how this little plant spent five years developing a strong root system to support its dramatic grow.

My assignment was to teach about the life of the farmer. *The Bamboo Effect* is more about the life of the farmer than it is about the life cycle of the bamboo. It was about what it takes to hold on to your Vision despite all obstacles and appearances of failure.

I was operating in my fifth year. It was time for me to go into the world and teach. It was time to share all the life lessons I had learned about being a farmer over my own life. My task was to draw from my own successes and failures. My challenges were varied: how I managed to survive being abandoned and getting a divorce; how I struggled to rear two sons as a single mother; how my youngest son's diagnosis of Autism forced me to change my career path. There was the pain of losing my home in a foreclosure and having our belongings tossed onto the curb as well as how my career path was forsaken to focus on teaching and advocating for the proper education of both of my sons.

Over a thirteen year span, I held jobs ranging from a part-time telemarketer selling the New York Times to an after school provider for the Campfire Boys/Girls Club. For a professional woman who was brought up in a Christian family that valued marriage and financial/educational success, it felt like I had hit rock bottom.

I could not give up on my dreams, despite all of the above setbacks. The small publishing company I founded in 1999 continued to complete its mission. With others coming on board later, we continued to help individuals accomplish their personal goals of becoming published authors. We have published nine books to date, including two of my own. At the same time, I held on to the deep assurance my life mission would manifest. My intention is to deliver a message of hope and love that is so powerful, it will be the cure for generations. *The Bamboo Effect* is about getting to your harvest time. It is about learning to experience life as "A Good Farmer."

Trust

Before you select your field and before you plant your first seed, you must understand the importance of trust. It is not enough to have faith that you can accomplish your dreams; you also must learn to trust. So what is the difference? Isn't faith and trust the same thing? No. Faith is a noun and trust is a verb. Think of faith as the power source necessary to operate trust. Faith is what you believe. Trust is taking what you believe and putting it into action.

We can have faith in our ability to write a book. We can have faith in our ability to start a new business. We can have faith in our ability to grow a bamboo farm. It will take trust to write your business plan. It will take trust to change scattered notes into a manuscript. It will take trust for a bamboo farmer to clear and plow his land.

How do we increase our level of trust? Start by having faith in the fundamental truth that your life began with a divine purpose. You came into existence with everything you needed to be successful. You are a fully-loaded factory model! You come equipped with a Global Position System (GPS) called Spirit. However, Spirit does not work unless activated. Push the "Faith" button to turn it on! Hit the "Trust" button to begin your journey.

Next, develop trust in the process and not the outcome. We learn most life lessons during the journey, not after we arrive at our destination. Think about it. Sometime during the fifth year the bamboo shoot *will* press the soil. A healthy plant is the desired outcome. The process is watering, fertilizing and nurturing the plant every day. Remember what you do today will determine your tomorrow. If you find yourself filled with worry or anxiety, it is a great indicator you are too concerned about the outcome. Shift your attention by becoming task oriented. Determine what you can accomplish right now, and then do it. One of my favorite prayers is "Spirit, allow me to do only that which is mine to do." I love this prayer because experience has taught me to *Trust*. I know if it is mine to do I have what it takes to "Get it done."

Appreciate Where You Are

As a young girl, I would often say "I can't wait until I grow up." My thoughts were that adults had more freedom than children. My mother's response to my statement was always the same "Don't wish your life away." It took years to grasp the meaning of her words of wisdom. You have to appreciate exactly where you are in life despite your hardships. No one likes to struggle. Learning to overcome difficulties is one of the ways we grow. In the case of the bamboo plant: Did the small plant sit inactive for four years, patiently waiting till the fifth year? The small plant was evolving itself beneath the soil by increasing its root system to make it strong enough to withstand its forthcoming external growth during the fifth year and beyond. We waste time wishing we could relive the past or fantasize about how much better we will be in the future. Appreciate what you have now. Take advantage of the opportunities in the present.

Decrease Your Recovery Time

Have you noticed how some people appear unmoved or undisturbed by a problem while everyone else involved in the situation are losing their composure? These individuals seem unshakable. What makes them so different? Chances are they have knowledge of two important facts. (1) Adversities and problems are a natural part of life. (2) It is more productive to focus on the solution rather than worry about the problem. Does that mean we should develop a pessimistic attitude? Should we go around expecting bad things to happen? We should not! However, if we acknowledge bad things can and will happen we are less likely to panic when they do. As you learn to embrace this simple reality, the occurrences of adversities will become less stressful. It is possible to train yourself to value the challenges as opportunities to create personal growth.

My friends often hear me say "My recovery time is better than when I began my journey." If you have ever participated in any physical exercise or ran a race, you will understand the meaning of recovery time. Once you finish an exercise of any kind, the body has to recover. The first time I finished a 5K race, it took me all day to recover. I remember going straight from the race to the gym to sit in the sauna. Later in the afternoon I took a long nap and was still tired. I was in bed before 9 p.m. that night. It took me forever to recover from pushing myself to finish one race. Well, as my workouts progressed, it took less and less time to recover.

After a year of participating in 5K runs, I was not thinking very much about recovering from the race. I was more concerned about recovering from the after parties that followed the events.

The same is true with facing any life challenges. Each time you come across a problem similar to one you had before, you should notice a decrease in the time it takes you to regain composure. A good farmer knows high winds and storms are going to happen. A good farmer knows there will be seasons of scorching hot days and droughts. There will also come times of floods that could wash away his crop in a single day. However, as he matures, he should begin to see a decrease in the time it takes him to regain his composure or to recover.

For example, the farmer has a set back and cannot get enough water to his crop. Sure, the first reaction might be "Oh, what am I going to do if I can't water my plants?" But that thought should be followed by all right let me see what changes have to be made to fix the problem so I will have enough water in the future. The length of time between the "What am I going to do?" and the possible solutions should shorten. You will recover faster from the initial shock of what "appears" to be adversities. You will soon recognize the uselessness in being in a state of "What am I going to do?"

It is far more beneficial to shift to "All right, the first thing I am going to do is..." See the difference? I have a three solution rule. If I am speaking with a person who is struggling with anything, I will offer them three possible ways of dealing with the issue. If the person finds holes in all three of the solutions, yet does not come up with counter solutions, it is a sign. The individual might be too focused on the problem and less focused on finding an answer to the problem. The key is practice, practice, practice. The more you get in the habit of looking for solutions, the more you will begin to see adversities as opportunities for growth.

Start using these techniques (1)Come up with your own three solutions; (2) look for the lessons you can learn from the adversity; and (3) use your words to make the problem temporary. It's simple. When you discuss the problem, say things such as "This is only temporary or I don't expect to have to deal with this for long." Words carry power; use them carefully.

Challenge Your Fears

Imagine the bamboo farmer, standing in the middle of an open field of nothingness. The only thing he totally possesses is his vision. This sole idea will provide for his family for years and years to come. Chinese bamboo plants require years to produce. It can take up to six years before he will reap his first harvest. He will have to wait a long time before he gets a complete return on his initial investment. After the first harvest, cutting will take place on an annual basis and can continue for up to 50 years. There is no way to take on such a risky task without getting a knot in your gut.

Can you identify with his fears? What a huge gamble to take a chance on your future. Picture the farmer carefully placing one tiny seed at a time into the ground and then sprinkling each mound of dirt with water. After he has planted the last seed, he stands in the middle of his field and sees nothing.

Amazingly, there is a cure for fear. It is action. If you want to accomplish anything, start by doing something even though you are feeling afraid. It is literally impossible to stand still while walking forward at the same time. Don't let fear paralyze your actions. It is okay to be honest about feeling afraid. Identifying and acknowledging personal fear(s) is the first step in overcoming it. Take action every day. It does not work if you do a little bit for a month then hide your head under the sand for the next two months.

The bamboo farmer has to be committed to succeed before he digs the first hole. You have to take the same approach to your vision. Take Action. The name of my company is Level Seven, developed around the importance of taking action. A level one is sitting on the sofa saying "One day I am going to do this or that." A level ten is working with unorganized plans and excessive distractions. A level seven is where things get accomplished; a level seven is making a commitment to do a minimum of one thing daily towards your dream. You do not fall asleep without completing one task. Level Seven Publishing has used this method on all of its books, including this one. The bottom line is to make every day count. Remember, feeling the fear and taking action despite fear separates those who have dreams from those who accomplish their dreams.

Develop Your Thoughts

Have you heard this quote? This quote is in numerous books. Why? Because the ability to control your thoughts is the magic key that unlocks your true potential. *The Bamboo Effect* cannot occur in your life without this important step. You have to change your thoughts to change your world. Although, it sounds like it is something that could take years. The change can occur as rapidly as an "Ah Ha" moment.

Once you grasp the fact that your thoughts are manifesting your destiny, your life will instantly transform. It does not take years to grasp this concept. It just takes paying close attention to your thoughts for a short period. Start by doing this simply exercise for a week.

Set a small notepad and pen next to your bed to record the first thoughts you have when you wake up. As soon as you open your eyes, what are your initial thoughts about your day? Do you say things such as Gosh, I wish I could stay in bed all day? Time to go to my crappy job. I am broke or my utilities company will turn off my service today. Once you begin recording your thoughts, it won't be long before you see a pattern. At the end of the week evaluate your notes. If your thoughts weigh more toward the negative, it is time to make changes.

Our thought patterns are similar to painting a picture on a canvas. The problem is most of us have become accustomed to using the dot-to-dot method of painting. We use the same pattern over and over again. We don't challenge ourselves to develop new techniques. We don't dare color outside of the lines. We just keep painting the same way year after year, producing the same drab life portrait. It takes courage to admit we are stuck. To create a beautiful bamboo field, the farmer has to look at nothing, yet try to see a vision of a thriving harvest. He has to overcome continually negative thoughts of nothingness. It's crazy to suggest you erase all past thoughts. We know it would be impossible to leave behind all old memories. It is possible to determine if your thoughts are serving you well or causing delays.

However, the fact is your thoughts are either bringing you closer to harvest day or moving you farther away. The great news is you can change the way you think. You have the power to record a new set of thoughts. How? By using one of these tools (1) scriptures, (2) affirmations, (3) mantra or (4) songs. It is not necessary to select just one of the four. You can use all of them or choose the one that works for you. It is a ritual for me to read a scripture every morning. I also enjoy reading the inspirational thoughts from the *Daily Word*. My favorite scripture is "I can do all things through Christ who strengthens me" (Philippians 4:13). Yes, it is a basic scripture which I adopted my freshman year of college. During the same period of time I began reciting "We are troubled on every side, yet not distressed;

we are perplexed, but not in despair" (2 Corinthians 4:8). I also used "What shall we say to these things? If God be for us, who can be against us" (Romans 8:31). I would write these scriptures on small index cards and tape them to my bathroom mirrors.

Years later I still use these powerful words to move me past thoughts of failure or insecurity. Do you have a song which inspires you? Sing it aloud. Singing is a soothing way to shift your thoughts, because music holds such healing power. Affirmations and mantras can be used to redirect your thoughts gently during moments of doubts. Once you have chosen ones that works for you, write it down and recite it while driving, exercising or while getting dressed for work. The fastest way to reprogram your thoughts is to replace your old worn out negative ones with new ones.

Re-Write Your Story

We all have one or two great stories we enjoy telling. For most people, one of the all-time favorites is their "life story." After all, it is the one they've had the most practice telling. What is your story? Let me hear it. Start with "Hello, my name is_____and this is my story." "Go ahead, I'll wait" - Katt Williams.

Does your story include a little bit of drama, disappointments, good days and sadness? Days when you felt on top of the world and days when you wanted to give up? Family members who were there for you and those who hurt you? Have you experienced the joy of holding a newborn and the pain of saying good-bye to cherished loved ones? Sounds like your life has been quite an adventure. Thank you for sharing. Now, allow me to share something with you: stop telling the same old story! Why? The answer is because our words are a powerful tool. If you keep telling the "Same Old Story," you will become just that...the same old story. The story we tell is the person we become. It does not matter if it's a great story; no one is listening. Well, except for maybe the people who are strapped in by a seatbelt while you tell it. Now, it does not mean you can never tell part(s) of your story. It just means when you tell it, make sure you are telling it from a different place in life. Don't allow years to go by with you stuck in the same place.

Several years ago, my decision to change my story resulted in me leaving a church. Relocating to a new church might not seem like a big deal to some of you, however, I grew up and reside in the southern region of the United States. It is not culturally uncommon to attend the same church for your entire life. I loved everything about being a member of this church. I respected the minister and his wife; I admired their daughter; I loved the choir, the biblical teachings; the people and the building. I left "my" church and took my sons with me. It was a very stressful life changing experience. What is the connection between changing to a new church and changing your life story? At the time, it meant freedom to grow and evolve into a new person.

Allow me to explain. When I became a member of this church, I was a happily married woman. My husband and I taught a Sunday school class together; we were active in the Military Ministry and attended marriage retreats. When my husband abandoned his family, it was shocking news to all who knew us, especially, the members of our church. Heck! It was shocking to me. The most difficult part was telling my story over and over again. Since, I could not make a public announcement from the pulpit or to take out an advertisement in the Sunday Bulletin, I had to re-cap the same story. My friends and church members were all concerned about me and the well-being of our two sons. It was understandable they wanted to assist me make heads or tails of what was happening. So, they often inquired about how we were doing.

Then one day, I heard myself telling

the same story. It made me uncomfortable. My husband and I separated four years prior to having to answer the same question. My story was beginning to sound like a made for *Lifetime* television movie. It was not a movie I wanted to watch repeatedly. I was ready to move forward. There was more to life than being a single mother rearing two boys on her own. I did not like being identified as the lovely lady who was struggling to get on her feet. Therefore, I located to another church. Attending a new church gave me the opportunity to stop telling the same old story. I began to meet new people. It was not long before I was learning new life skills. I did not have to answer the same questions. Yes, there were times when I shared information about my broken marriage. It was shared only as a part of my life journey, not my entire journey. I was not telling the same old story from the same old place in life. I was moving forward. I was writing a new chapter in my life. I had begun working on a new vision for my life. In fact, one of the first steps I took after attending a workshop at my new church was to develop a "Vision Plan."

No farmer can become successful if he spends a life time sharing about the flood that destroyed his bamboo field twenty years ago. Don't you think it is time to move forward? Start by writing a vision plan for your life. The quickest way to begin making positive changes in your life is to write down your plan. Napoleon Hill in his book *Think and Grow Rich* makes it clear the key to success is a well written *Vision Plan*. Once you have your plan, you can develop strategies to take action. Place your plan somewhere you can read it daily. Use your plan to set mini daily goals.

A successful farmer understands and embraces the power of a well-written vision plan. Habakkuk 2:2: "And the Lord answered me, and said, write the vision, and make it plain upon tablets, that he may run that readeth it."

Know Your Self-Worth

Whatever you think about yourself, others will usually co-sign it. You have to see the value of the contributions you make in life. Do you take time to celebrate your tiny successes? Do you appreciate your individual gifts? Most of time, we allow parents, teachers, ministers, friends, family members and bosses to determine our worth. A great place to start is to evaluate payment for your gifts. When was the last time you negotiated your salary? Several years ago a former employer stated to me "I am paying you $20.00 dollars per hour. I feel as if I am paying you too much." It was very offensive to hear someone under appreciate my worth, especially considering the amount of time and labor I was putting into the job. I said nothing. I continued to work for her despite the knowledge of how little value she was placing on my service. Thankfully my inner self knew better. What if I had bought into her belief about me? What if I allowed her limited views to become my views? Chances are I would not have had the courage to live life beyond her expectations, and you would not be reading this book.

Make the decision to evaluate your skill level. Let's look at the life of the bamboo farmer. What would happen if he allowed others to determine his worth? If others judged him on how fast he could grow a crop, he would be a complete failure. If he was measured by his patience, determination and dedication to a task, well he would be viewed as the ultimate success. Getting bias results is the trap of allowing others to set the standard for measuring your worth. Develop the habit of doing a self-evaluation. It is up to you to know when you are on task or if you need to make changes. A dear friend always reminds me of a basic fact. When you allow others to measure you against them, there is a high chance they will measure your skills less than they measure themselves.

Giving Without Expectations

Several months after losing my job, I decided to do something I had not done for quite some time. I made the decision to buy myself a bouquet of fresh flowers. Those who are close to me know I absolutely love flowers. I get great pleasure from working in my yard with plants. The other thing my friends will tell you is that I am allergic to most plants. They get a big laugh out of me riding home with the windows down because the pollen from the plants makes my eyes itch and burn. So, despite my allergies or the fact making the purchase might mean I did not have enough gas money for the week, I decided to splurge on myself.

Imagine my surprise when I discovered the local food store near my home had a selection of lovely bouquets marked down to half price. Although some of the buds were in full bloom and would not last more than a couple of days, they were beautiful. The florist explained every Monday the store marked down their flowers for quick sale. I had been depriving myself of something I loved when I could have gotten it for fewer than five dollars. This day was just getting better and better. Maybe it was a sign life was about to shift for me and my sons.

As I was leaving the store with my fresh flowers in hand, I saw a lady attempting to push her buggy to her car. She was an elderly lady with a beautiful pink and green scarf wrapped around her head. A closer look revealed a small oxygen tank in her buggy. I rushed over to assist her. She was more than grateful for my help. She shared she had just gotten out of the hospital. She had come to the grocery store to purchase soup and crackers. Her adult children lived out of town and were due to arrive the following day. I removed the things from her buggy placing them on her back seat. What stood out about this lady was her pleasing disposition. She was apparently not feeling well; she was alone and challenged by doing for herself despite the obvious need for assistance. She was smiling and mustered up the energy to show her gratitude toward me. As I was walking away, it hit me. I turned around and said "Ma'am, these flowers are for you". Tears instantly welled up in her eyes as I placed the flowers in the passenger's seat. I only smiled and said, "You are welcome."

That was the beginning of my flower ministry. For the next year, I would purchase flowers at the local store in the marked down section and give the bouquct away when someone moved or inspired me. Many times, I barely made it out of the store. One of my favorite times was when I encountered a young man in the store who was sharing with anyone who would listen about his wife having their first child. He was ecstatic. As he was checking out he made this simple statement, "Gosh, a woman does a lot for a man when she gives birth to his son. It makes you want to do anything for her." I could not check out fast enough so I could chase him down in the parking lot to tell him I was giving him the bouquet of fresh flowers for his wife. He did not tear up. He actually cried. He could barely get out a thank you. He had just started a new job and had been trying to figure out how to buy something for his wife.

My flower ministry was something I did not share with anyone. It was my private way of telling God thank you. It gave me joy to see the smiles on the individual's faces when giving them the flowers. It did not dawn on me how important my Monday flower ministry had become until one Sunday I was sitting in church without a dime to my name. I mean not one single solitary dime. As I began to pray to God, my silent prayer even surprised me. "God, I have nothing to give today. I just ask you to provide for me enough money to buy my flowers tomorrow." I had grown accustomed to God providing for my children and myself. I wanted to make someone's day a little brighter with my gift of flowers. I realized giving was helping me cope with my own struggles. It was my way of feeling like I always had enough. So I asked to make sure I had money to share my love of flowers with someone the following day.

Later that night, I received a phone call from one of my dear friends. She asked if I had enough gas to meet her in about an hour. She wanted to meet, of all places, in front of the store where I purchased my weekly flowers. My friend was standing beside her car when I arrived; she explained she was rushing to get to another engagement. She went into her wallet before handing me a $100.00 dollar bill. She shared with me that spirit had instructed her to give me the money. This time I cried. I cried all the way back home. I was so thankful for such an awesome gift. I heard my inner voice say "I saw every flower you gave out and blessings will rain upon your life for every single petal for what you gave was love."

It is important to give your best even when it feels like you have nothing to share. As a real bamboo farmer, you will have periods of time when there appears to be nothing to do. Heck, you might have to wait five years for your dream to manifest. Don't spend extra time sitting around worrying or distressed; volunteer to help an elderly person, sweep someone's yard, walk your neighbor's dog or give out flowers to complete strangers. Being unemployed or underemployed can never stop love. Showing and sharing love is a very inexpensive gift with the greatest return on your investment.

Granddaddy's Car

One of the greatest challenges is seeing beyond our current situation. It is so easy for the day to day to become the week to week and the year to year. Why? Because when you become accustomed to doing anything long enough, it will develop into a routine. A habit is a process you have routinely done until it has become second nature. All habits are not bad. The habit of practicing daily hygiene will take you far. The habit of washing your hands before you eat or always saying "please" and "thank you" are excellent social skills. What I am speaking about are the habits that prevent you from making necessary changes in your life. If you want to turn your adversities into tools of growth, you have to change the way you look at things.

My dearest friend Camellia shared a story with me numerous years ago. Camellia has a wonderful sense of humor. I enjoy a good laugh, so we have great conversations. The story she told was about growing up as a small girl in Memphis. One of the things she recalled vividly was going to spend time at her grandparent's home. During her visits, she and her cousin would play outside in the front yard. On one occasion, while they were playing outside, a neighborhood dog came over and began to chase them. She and her cousin were running in circles around her grandparent's home yelling and crying while trying to get away from the dog. Suddenly, Camellia made the decision to climb on top of her granddaddy's car. Once she was safely on top of the car, she was able to watch the dog continue to chase her cousin and wonder why he was franticly running around the house in circles. She was also thinking how silly he was not to just stop and jump on top of the car with her. We both laughed at her childhood memory.

Until one day we looked at the deeper message in the experience. If you want to make changes in life, you have to change the way you look at things. Often you have to remove yourself from the situation. If you cannot move physically you have to move mentally. So "Get on top of your Granddaddy's" car became a mantra for us. If she called me complaining about the unfairness of her work I would remind her she needed to get on top of her granddaddy's car.

If you are unemployed or working a job for far less than you deserve, it's time you got on top of your granddaddy's car. Once you are there, you need to do the following steps:

(1)   Take a deep breath and celebrate how much safer you feel. See, the reason Camellia was able to rationalize her situation was because she was safe. She had removed herself from any danger she might have felt earlier.

(2)   Access your situation from a different position: As Camellia was sitting on the

car she could easily see the dog was not dangerous at all. The dog was panting with his tongue hanging out and probably thought it was a friendly game of catch me if you can.

(3) Plan your next move. The new way of looking at life will give you the ability to make better plans.

The moral of the story is a simple one. If you change the way you look at things, the way things look will change. So the next time you are confronted with a negative co-worker, stuck in heavy traffic or standing in the employment line, " Get on top of your Granddaddy's car" and appreciate the new view.

Give up Control

There are a number of areas in our lives where we are totally without control. It does not matter how much you want to change a circumstance. You cannot make it happen yourself. In the case of the bamboo farmer, it does not matter how many times a day he waters, nurtures or fertilizes his plants, the harvest will not come until it is ready. As you work towards your vision, be prepared to face situations that render you powerless.

During my early twenties, I wanted to join the Air Force to see the world. My only hesitation was my great-grand mother was an elderly woman in her eighties. I could not imagine the pain of losing her while I was away on active duty. One day I shared with my great-grandmother, my reason for not joining the service. Shaking her head, she made this statement, "Well, if you were sitting next to my bed when God called me home, could you stop him?" She went on to share there are some things in life you cannot control. It was a powerful message. I joined the Air Force Reserves the following summer. My great-grandmother lived to be 95.

Begin by admitting you cannot control everything. It is the first step to Alcoholic Anonymous and various other treatments for conquering addictions. By surrendering your persistent need to hold on to power, you will begin to get in touch with the TRUE SOURCE, Spirit, who has the power to direct and guide your life.

Surround Yourself with Like-minded Farmers

"Birds of a feather flock together" is more than an old wives tale. I am going to take it as a proven fact. We develop habits, attitudes and behaviors similar to the people we associate with the most. If you surround yourself with successful people, it will be easier to work for your own success. Hang around a group of individuals whose primary goal every day is complaining or drinking/drugging to escape life, and before long you too will develop the habit of wasting time. Surround yourself with great role models. Your mentor will not seek you out; you must seek them.

It is important to share ideas with people who understand the power of having a vision. Even though they may have different goals and plans, the fact that they have a plan is mandatory. Separate yourself from naysayers: they are not a part of the success package. You can be assured that naysayers are more than willing to tell the bamboo farmer how much time he is wasting. It would be easy for outsiders to feel the farmer was watering piles of dirt year in and year. Make it a practice to select people who not only support your ideas but who will also help you. The last thing you need is to spend unnecessary time convincing others you have a viable dream. I once read this statement, "Walk with the tallest or walk along."

Tap into Your Creativity

When my son was young, I shared with him that during the "Great Depression" there were three types of people: (1) There were people jumping out of windows, (2) There were people being pushed out of windows, and (3) There were people designing, building and selling new windows. I told this story to my son to emphasize the lesson of being creative during a crisis. When I lost my job, my initial reaction was to panic. And that is what I did; I panicked. Sometimes we have to be pushed to take on a new direction.

How was it possible for me to fail to use the very lesson I had taught? Easily, by forgetting to tap into my own creativity. It happens to the best of us. We live in an instant gratification society. Most of us have become accustomed to buying everything the moment we want or need it. It is rare to find individuals who cook dinner every single day of the week instead of pulling up at the drive-thru or individuals who make/sew their own clothing versus heading to the nearest mall.

As a society, we rarely set aside time for creative things such as dancing, singing, painting or writing. Your natural talents might be the quickest way to your abundance. If you could speak to any of the numerous self-made millionaires about how they achieved, most would tell you they rediscovered a skill or a talent that they already possessed.

Perhaps you've always loved making cupcakes, crafting purses, hosting parties, or telling jokes. We are each born with gifts that set us apart from one another. The successful millionaires merely discovered and developed ways to make money by doing the thing that they loved. One of the most traumatic days of my young life happened when I was in the fourth grade. My teacher gave us the assignment to write about our talent. I cried on my walk home. I was so upset because I could not think of one talent to write about. I could not sing, or dance or paint or bake cookies. I did not have a talent. The moment I walked in the house my mother asked me what was wrong with me. Mothers have a way of knowing things way ahead of time. When I told her about the assignment I stated "the only thing I can do is talk".

She stated "Melondy, that is your talent. Everyone cannot talk as well as you can." Wow! Thank God for mothers! Today when someone says to me "Gosh, Melondy, you talk too much." My response is "I make my living talking. People pay me to talk." It is indeed a talent I can take to the bank.

Take time to tap into your inner creativity. If you want a better life, you have to create it. Don't sit around waiting for someone else to create it for you! Design and build your own window or be prepared to jump or get pushed!

Become Courageous

Have you ever had one of those days when nothing seemed to go right? One of those days when your faith was shaken? One of those days when your trust was depleted? One of those days when despite your best efforts, you could not control your negative thoughts?

Did you feel like your only choice was to give up? Throw in the towel? Walk away from it all? Well, I was experiencing one of those days just described. Then I read this status update on Facebook:

"At the Cancer Clinic with Sandra Dunbar, my wife. She is a warrior & we will be victorious over this & other things that have been happening. To God Be the Glory."

Although I have never had the pleasure of meeting Sandra Dunbar, her husband, Sylvester, is my big brother. He is a member of Omega Psi Phi (Delta Eta Chapter). When I read his status three things happened: (1) I canceled my one of those days pity party; (2) I was inspired by Sylvester's willingness to share their journey and (3) I was motivated by Sandra without even knowing her. I know the phenomenal role we as women play in the lives of our families.

So what is courage? Webster defines courage as "the ability to do something that frightens one." Therefore, when Sylvester described Sandra as a "Warrior," my first thought was a warrior is a very powerful word. It takes a great deal of courage to be a warrior.

See, a warrior is not a person who fights a single battle, then collects all of their medals and goes home. A warrior engages in ongoing combat(s) and has a high degree of courage and skill. Did you note the "s" on the end of the word combat? Sylvester described his wife as a warrior with the knowledge, skill and courage to be victorious.

As a result of reading Sylvester's post about Sandra's courage, I added this chapter. A bamboo farmer has to have courage. How else can he face the uncertainties of growing a crop? Farmers have little to no control over the elements of nature. Therefore, they must possess a great deal of faith and trust in the ONE who controls everything, God! Think about it, if a farmer's crop is in the path of a tornado, his only recourse is to get out of the way. He has no power to stop the wind and the rain. He has to remain faithful through the storm and access the damages afterward. If he lacks the courage to be flexible and bend with ongoing changes, he will break. The farmer must have the courage to begin again and again and again. Just like the warrior who at times must prepare for the next battle before the current one ends. Without courage, it only takes a single one of those days experience to create failure for both the farmer and the warrior.

Let's be honest: this is true for all of us. Life has a way of catching up with us from time to time. It can knock us to our knees. However, the beautiful thing is knowing that "Courage is Contagious." It is almost impossible to be in the presence of someone being courageous and not get inspired. Therefore, keep your eyes, ears and hearts open because you never know where you might encounter an act of courage.

Be Tenacious

Once you have a well-written plan, you have to become tenacious. As I was tumbling rapidly towards the bottom, it became clear I did not have a plan "A" or "B." The only plans for my life connected to the mercy of others. My previous employer had plans for **her** company. It later became apparent those plans did not include me. So what happened? I was fired and pushed out the nest. She owed me no explanation for her decision. It did not matter if it was unfair or justifiable. Guess what? In retrospect, I see that was the best move she could have made on my behalf. It forced me to look at how much of a victim I had become. Like most Americans, I was waking up every day leaving the plans of my life up to someone else to make. Is this the way you are spending your days? Trust me! There is a long line of individuals who can't wait to give instructions on what you should or should not be doing with your life.

Taking responsibility of your life takes tenacity. If you fail, you have no one to blame but yourself. If you have your vision plan, it is easier to dismiss the naysayers or those currently referred to as "Haters."

So what is tenacity? It is the quality or fact of being able to grip something firmly. Do you want to see your vision manifest? Well you had better be prepared to hold on and stay focused regardless of the circumstances. Take time to study the list of synonyms for the word tenacity. The list contains words such as persistence, determination, perseverance, doggedness, strength of purpose, purposefulness, staunchness, steadfastness, staying power, endurance, stamina, stubbornness, intransigence obstinacy, obduracy, pertinacity. "The bamboo farmer latches on to his vision with the tenacity of a bulldog."

After you have become tenacious about what you **will** accomplish, it is mandatory to become extremely selective about sharing your vision plan. It takes energy to bring your dream to life. It also takes energy to convince others to believe in your plan. So why invest the time in trying to get others to believe in your dream? Share it only with those who will nurture and support your vision. Having active support is why joining an Accountability or Mastermind group is an excellent tool to increase your chance for success.

Prepare For the Unexpected

There is one element of success, which is often overlooked; it is preparing for the unexpected. This final lesson is the first step in manifesting your dream. It is only mentioned last because it combines all of the previous lessons. After you have spent endless days, months and years laboring your vision, one day it will happen. You arise early in the morning; pray; mediate; pick up your tools and head out the door to care for and nurture your dream. Then, the unexpected occurs: instead of the same piles of dirt there is a tiny green sprout peeking through the soil. It's your "Fifth Year." All of your hard work and determination has finally paid off. Can you just imagine the complete feeling of satisfaction? The overwhelming pride and joy of being able to stand at the edge of your field and see life coming forth right before your very eyes.

This my friend is the "Bamboo Effect." The moment when you become an overnight success. Oh, it will appear to be an overnight victory to almost everyone. The people on the outside will have forgotten how long you have been on your journey. They won't remember the day you planted your first seed. Only those in your hand-selected Mastermind group have witnessed your tears of frustration and fear. Sadly, most of your friends wrote you off years ago, when you refused to give up your crazy idea of growing a Bamboo crop or starting your own business or graduating from college, etc. Therefore, outsiders will misinterpret the truth. This moment to you is not a complete surprise. It is a moment you have been preparing, striving and anticipating to come for many years. There is an old saying: "It is better to be prepared and not have an opportunity than to have an opportunity and not be prepared."

We have all heard stories of authors having their first novel selected for Oprah's book club. It is not luck. The author prepared; then came the unexpected call from Oprah. One of my favorite rags to riches stories is Landau Eugene Murphy,

Jr. He appeared on the television show *American's Got Talent.*

Mr. Murphy was a gentleman who washed cars for a living. His outer appearance quickly stereotyped him as a "Rapper" or R & B singer. When he began singing, he sounded like Frank Sinatra. Landau won the competition. Winning the contest is an excellent example of the Bamboo Effect. Did his success happen overnight? Seemingly, yes. In actuality, no. He prepared for the unexpected. Can you picture him singing and washing cars for years? Landau Eugene Murphy Jr. now travels and performs on stages across the country. Yes, just like the tiny bamboo plant that can reach 90 feet in less than six weeks, Landau was launched into his vision.

This book is not about having to wait five years or ten or even two years to manifest your vision. Today is your Fifth Year...now grow!

www.ingramcontent.com/pod-product-compliance
Lightning Source LLC
LaVergne TN
LVHW021547080426
835509LV00019B/2886

9 780970 942364